PIANO
VOCAL
GUITAR

Rare

SELENA GOMEZ

ISBN 978-1-5400-8904-5

Visit Hal Leonard Online at
www.halleonard.com

Contact Us:
Hal Leonard
7777 West Bluemound Road
Milwaukee, WI 53213
Email: info@halleonard.com

In Europe, contact:
Hal Leonard Europe Limited
42 Wigmore Street
Marylebone, London, W1U 2RN
Email: info@halleonardeurope.com

In Australia, contact:
Hal Leonard Australia Pty. Ltd.
4 Lentara Court
Cheltenham, Victoria, 3192 Australia
Email: info@halleonard.com.au

RARE

Words and Music by SELENA GOMEZ,
MADISON LOVE, NOLAN LAMBROZA,
SIMON ROSEN and BRETT McLAUGHLIN

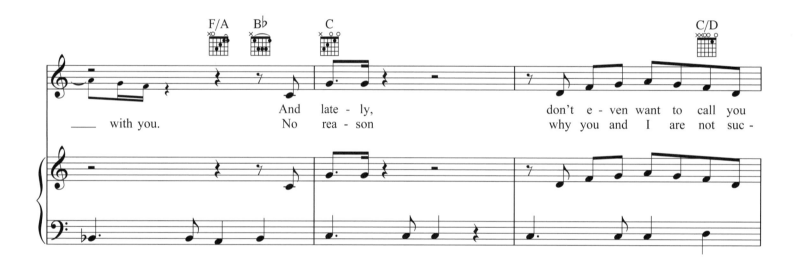

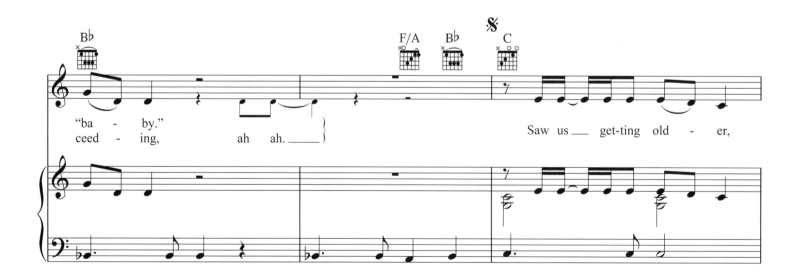

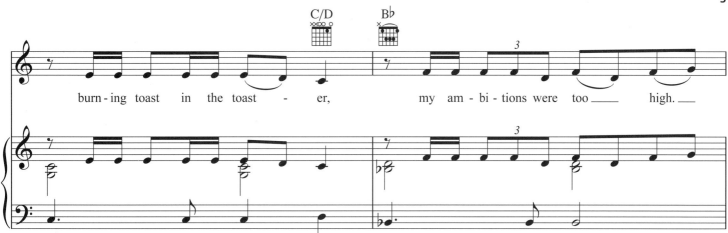

burn-ing toast in the toast - er, my am - bi - tions were too high.

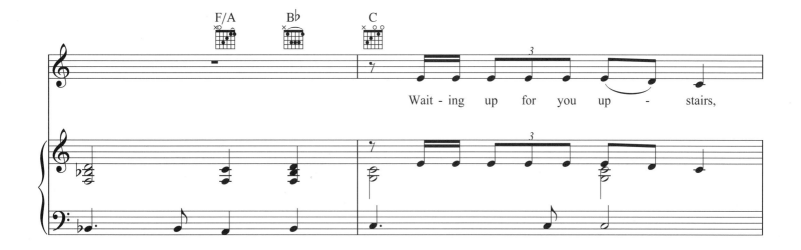

Wait - ing up for you up - stairs,

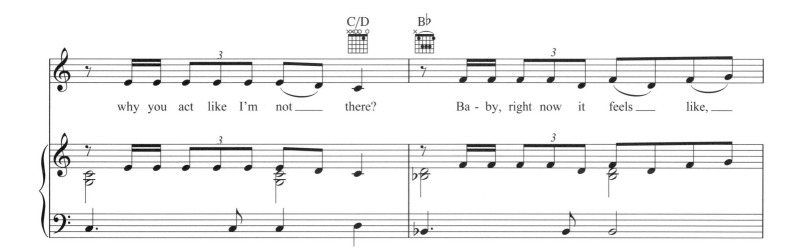

why you act like I'm not there? Ba - by, right now it feels like,

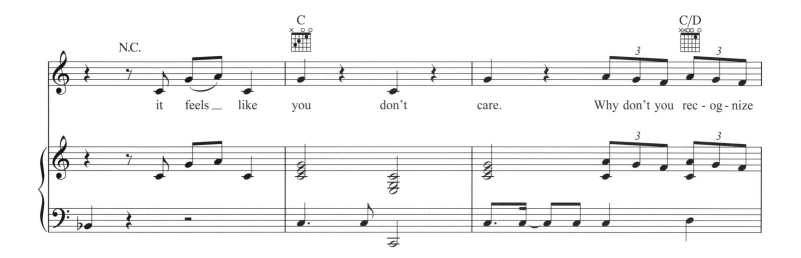

it feels like you don't care. Why don't you rec - og - nize

I'm so rare? _____ Al - ways

there, you don't do the same for me, that's not fair. _____ I don't

have it all, ___ I'm not claim - ing to ___ but I know that I'm

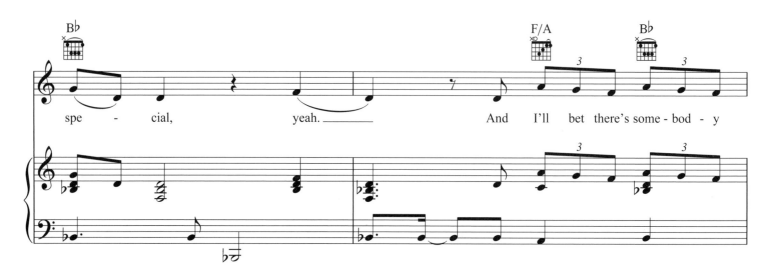

spe - cial, yeah. _____ And I'll bet there's some - bod - y

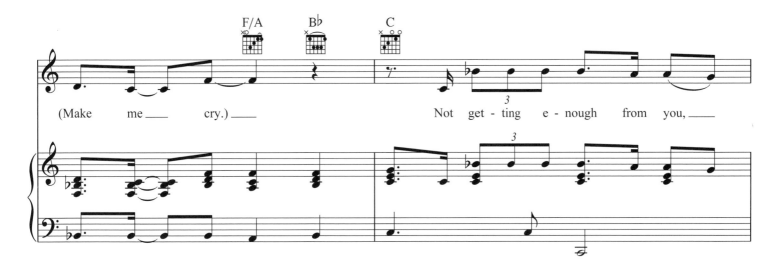

D.S. al Coda

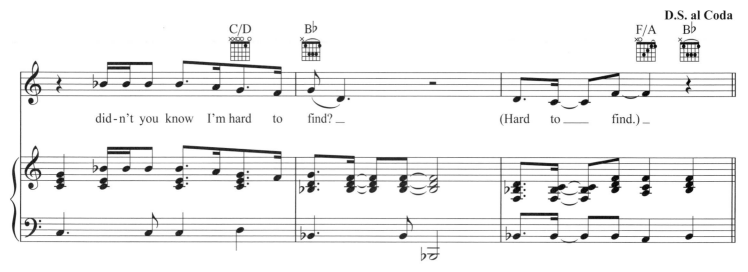

did-n't you know I'm hard to find? ___ (Hard to ___ find.) ___

CODA

Ooh yeah. So rare.
(Ah, ___ ah. ___

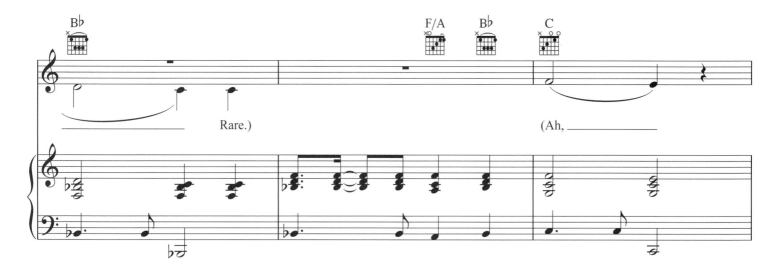

Rare.) (Ah, ___

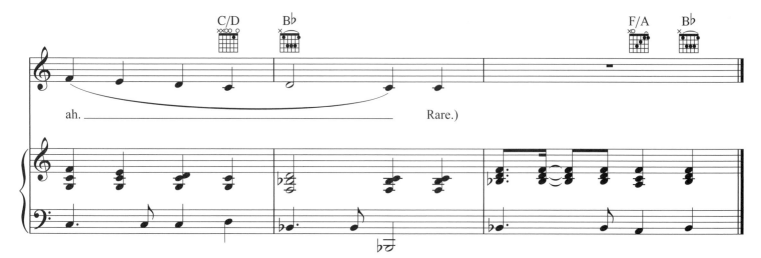

ah. ___ Rare.)

LOOK AT HER NOW

Words and Music by SELENA GOMEZ,
IAN KIRKPATRICK, JULIA MICHAELS
and JUSTIN TRANTER

Moderate Dance tempo

* Recorded a half step higher.

his too, till he had an - oth - er. Oh god, when she found out,

trust lev - els went way down. Of course __ she was sad, but now she's

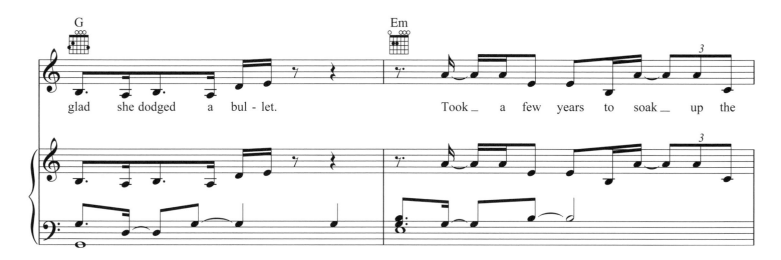

glad she dodged a bul - let. Took __ a few years to soak __ up the

tears, but look at her now. __ Watch her go. Mm mm mm, mm mm mm, mm mm.

To Coda ⊕

Wow, look at her now. __ Fast nights, that got him.

That new life was his prob - lem. Not say'n' she was per - fect;

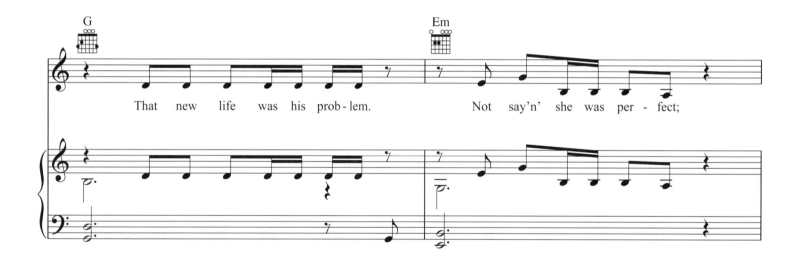

still re - grets that mo - ment, like that night. Was - n't wrong, was - n't right.

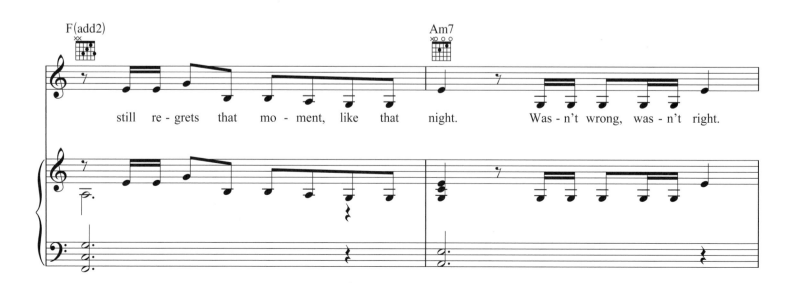

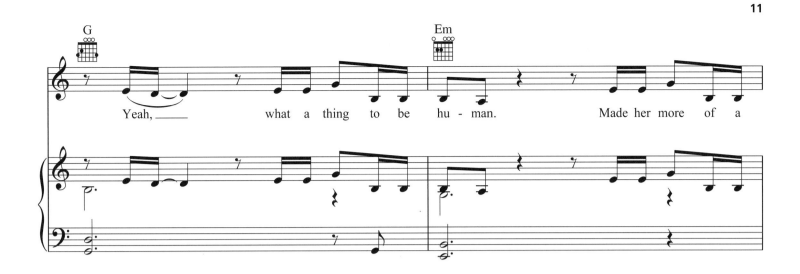

Yeah, _____ what a thing to be hu-man. Made her more of a

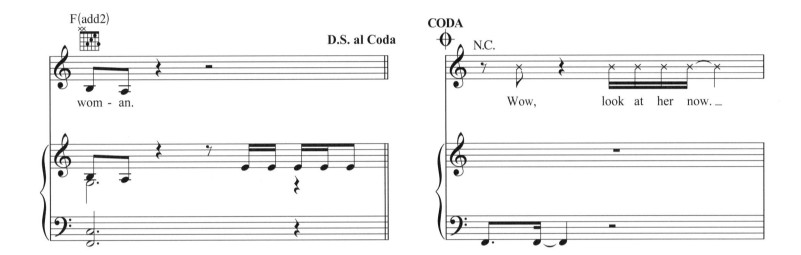

D.S. al Coda **CODA**

F(add2) Em N.C.

wom-an. Wow, look at her now. _

Am7

Wow, look at her now. _

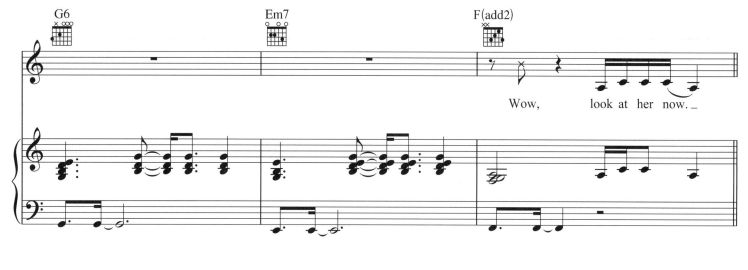

Wow, look at her now. _

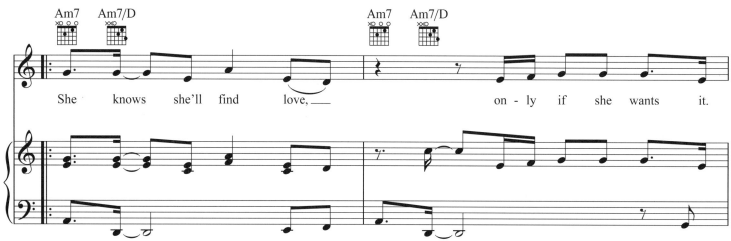

She knows she'll find love, ___ on-ly if she wants it.

1.
She knows _ she'll find love. ___
She knows _ she'll find love, ___

2.
on the up from the way down. Look at her now. Watch her go!

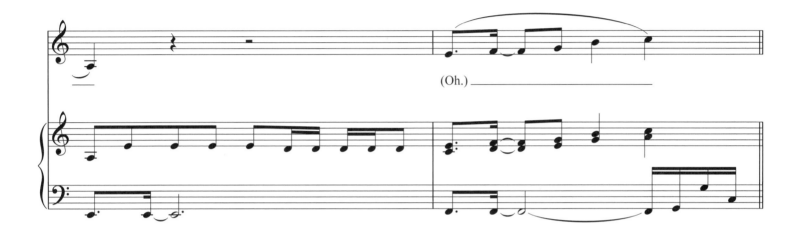

(Oh.)

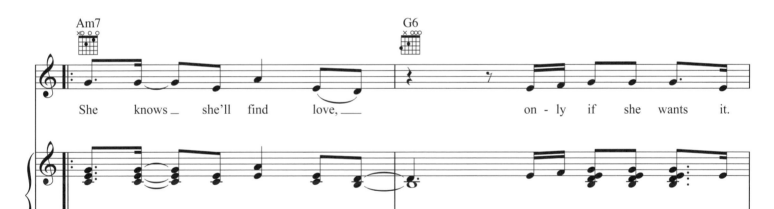

She knows __ she'll find love, __ on-ly if she wants it.

She knows __ she'll find love. __ Look at her now, yeah. Look at her now. __

DANCE AGAIN

Words and Music by SELENA GOMEZ,
ROBIN FREDRIKSSON, MATTIAS LARSSON,
JUSTIN TRANTER and CAROLINE AILIN

Moderately

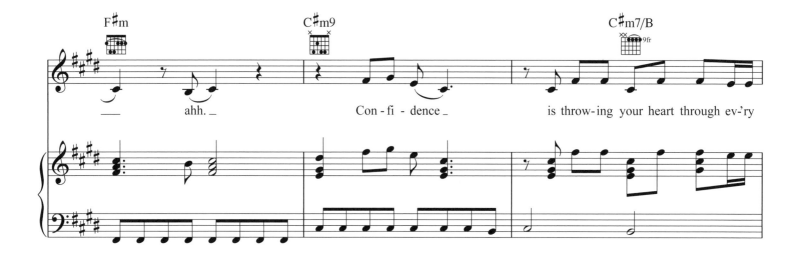

trau-ma's in re-mis - sion. No, I don't need per - mis - sion. __ Feels so, feels so, feels so good to

dance __ a - gain. __ Feels so, feels so, feels so good to dance __ a - gain. __

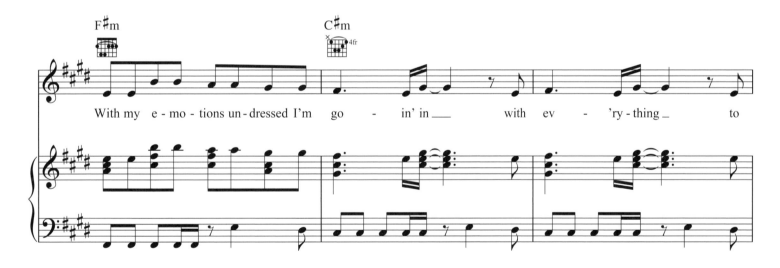

With my e - mo - tions un-dressed I'm go - in' in ___ with ev - 'ry - thing __ to

dance __ a - gain. __ Feels so, feels so, feels so good. Vul - ner -'ble __

ain't ea - sy, be - lieve me, but I go there, mmm, __ ahh. __ It's like I'm

ten feet tall. __ I'm high off the weight off of my shoul - ders, mmm, __

__ ahh. __ I kick start the rhy - thm, all the trau - ma's in re - mis - sion. No, I

don't need per - mis - sion. I kick-start my sys - tem. When I

D.S. al Coda

speak, my bod-y lis-tens. I know what I'm miss-in'. Feels so, feels so, feels so good to

Ooh, _____ ahh, ooh, _____ I'm feel-in',

Ooh, _____ ahh, ooh, _____ me a-gain. Ooh, _____ ahh,

ooh, _____ feels so good to dance __ a-gain. Ahh,

feels so, feels so, feels so good.
So, so ___ so good.

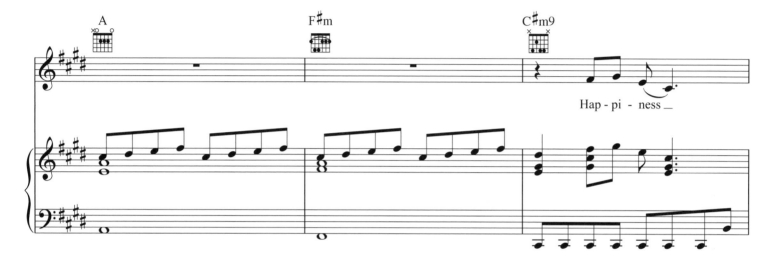

Hap - pi - ness ___

ain't some-thin' you sit back and you wait for.
Feels so, feels so, feels so good to

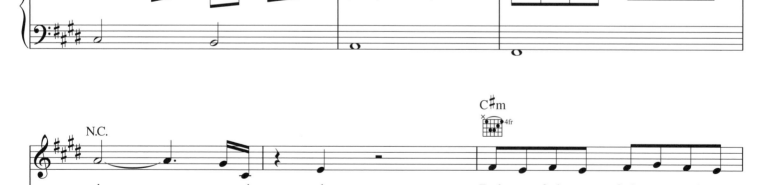

dance ___ a- gain, uh.
Feels so, feels so, feels so good to

dance _ a - gain. _ With my e - mo - tions un-dressed I'm go - in' in ___ with

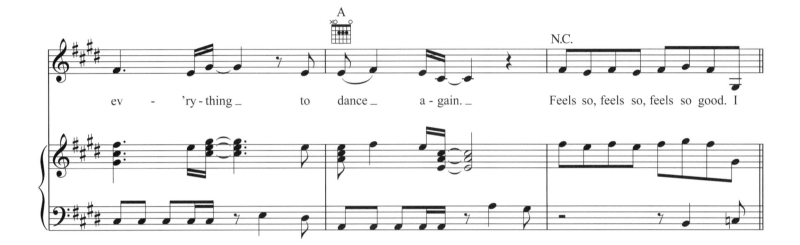

ev - 'ry-thing _ to dance _ a - gain. _ Feels so, feels so, feels so good. I

kick-start the rhy-thm, all the trau-ma's in re-mis-sion. Ooh, _____ ahh,

umm. _____ I feels so, feels so, feels so good. _____

LOSE YOU TO LOVE ME

Words and Music by SELENA GOMEZ,
JUSTIN TRANTER, JULIA MICHAELS,
ROBIN FREDRIKSSON and MATTIAS LARSSON

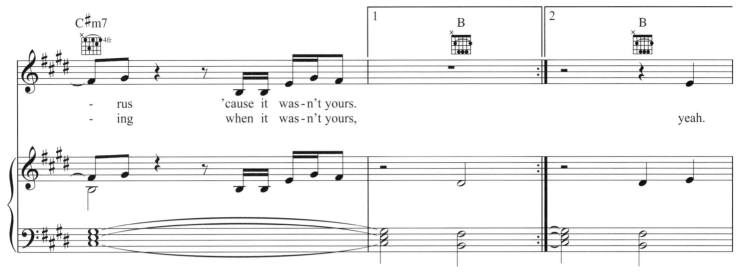

-rus   'cause it was-n't yours.
-ing   when it was-n't yours,   yeah.

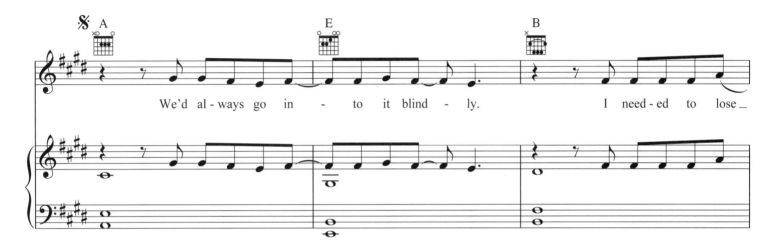

We'd al-ways go in - to it blind - ly.   I need-ed to lose _

_ you to find _ me.   This dance, it was kill - ing me soft - ly.

I need-ed to hate ___ you to love _ me, yeah.   To love, love, yeah, to

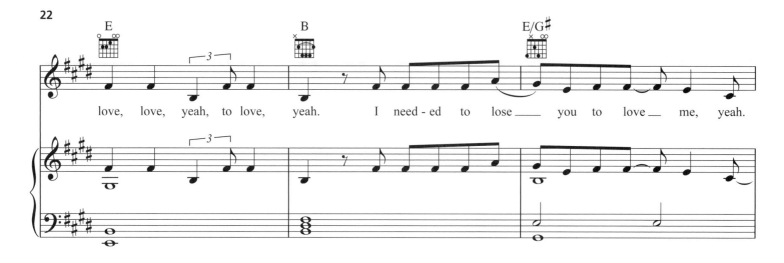

love, love, yeah, to love, yeah. I need-ed to lose ___ you to love ___ me, yeah.

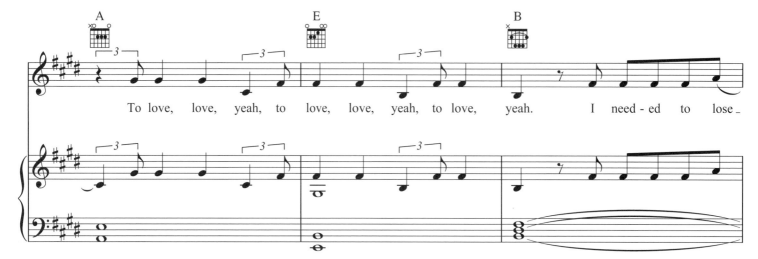

To love, love, yeah, to love, love, yeah, to love, yeah. I need-ed to lose ___

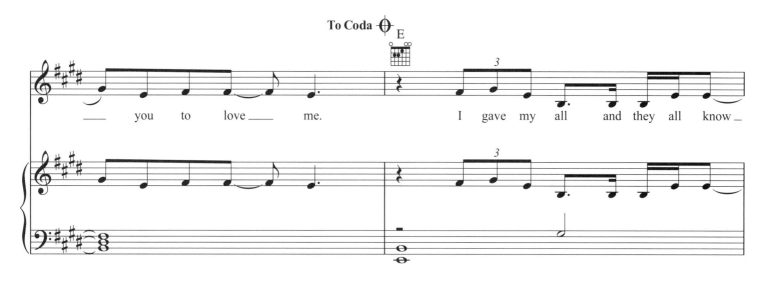

To Coda E

___ you to love ___ me. I gave my all and they all know ___

F#m7   C#m7

___ it. Then you tore me down and now it's show -

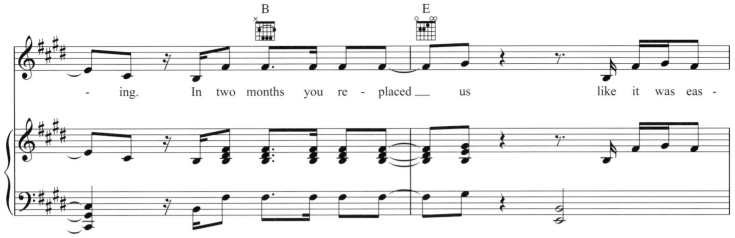

- ing. In two months you re - placed __ us like it was eas -

D.S. al Coda

y. Made me think I de - served __ it in the thick of heal - ing, yeah.

CODA

You prom - ised the world and I fell for it.

I put you first and you a - dored __ it. Set fires to my for -

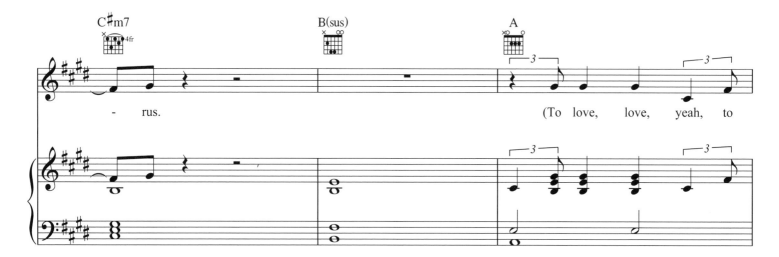

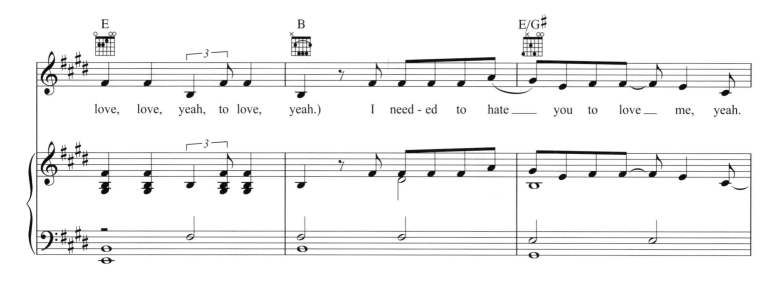

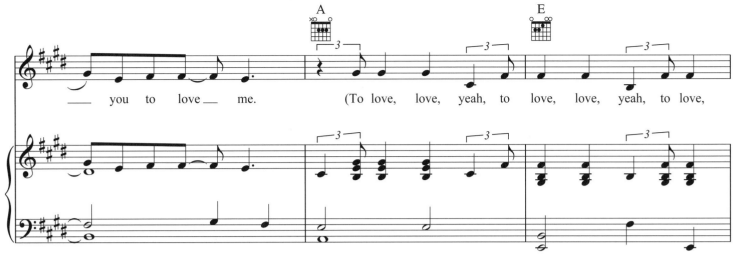

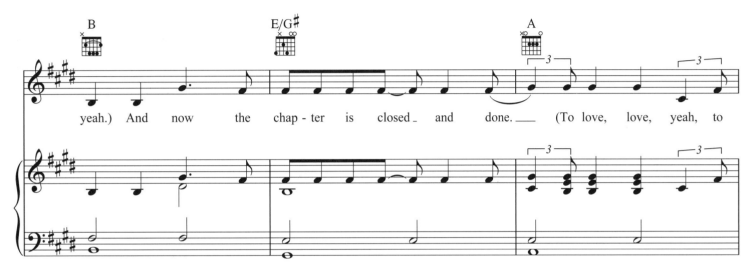

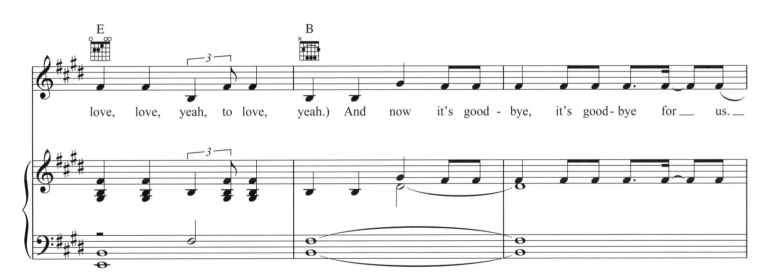

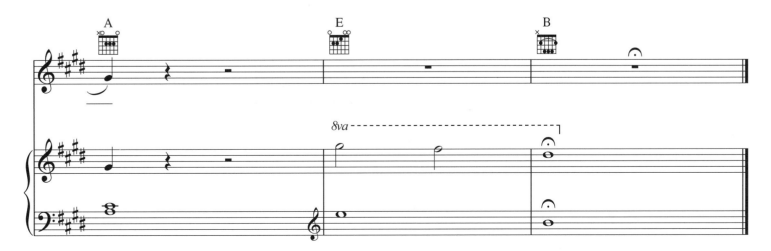

RING

Words and Music by SELENA GOMEZ,
NOLAN LAMBROZA, JULIE FROST,
SEAN DOUGLAS, BREYAN ISAAC
and DAVID CIENTE

Reggae-flavored Pop

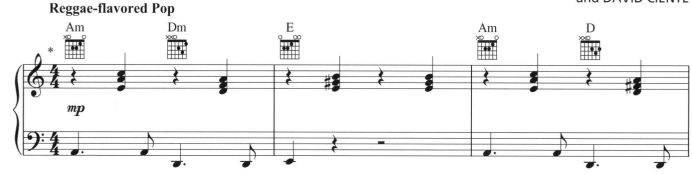

You all in your feel- ings, ba- by, all in- to me.

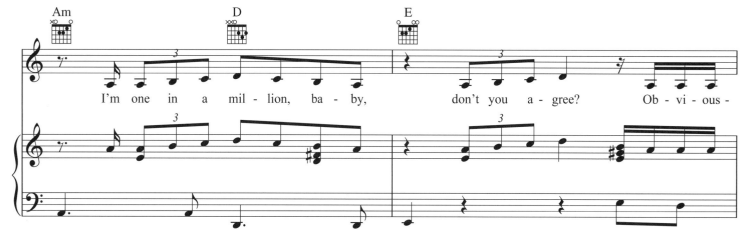

I'm one in a mil- lion, ba- by, don't you a- gree? Ob- vi- ous-

ly, you know, __ I'm a- ware of that. I'm break- ing hearts __ like a heart at- tack.

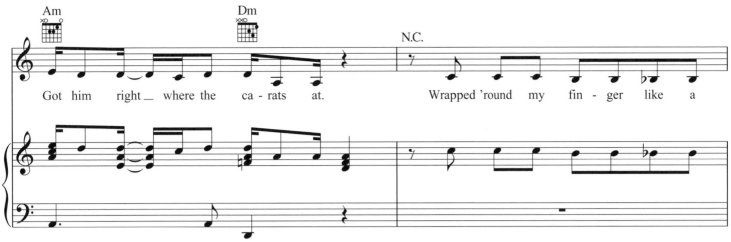

Got him right __ where the ca - rats at. Wrapped 'round my fin - ger like a

ring, ring, ring. They just like pup - pets on a string, string, string.

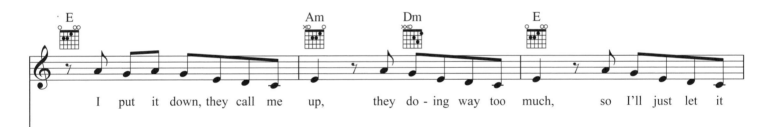

I put it down, they call me up, they do - ing way too much, so I'll just let it

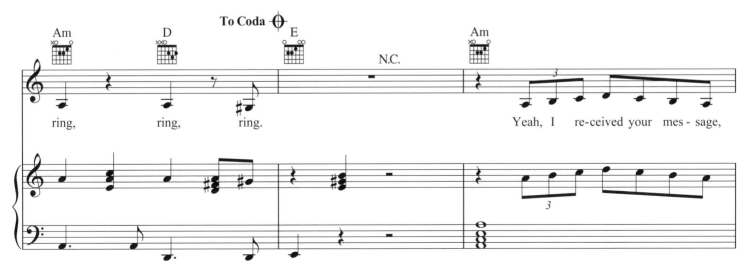

To Coda

ring, ring, ring. Yeah, I re - ceived your mes - sage,

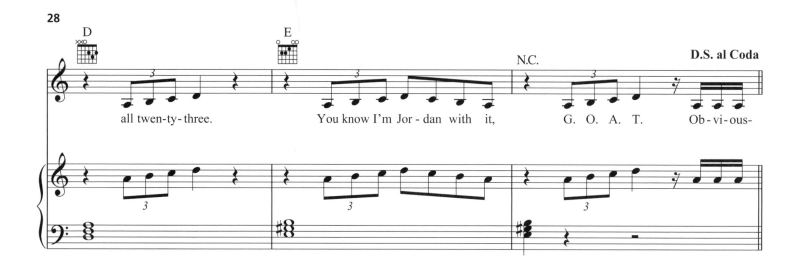

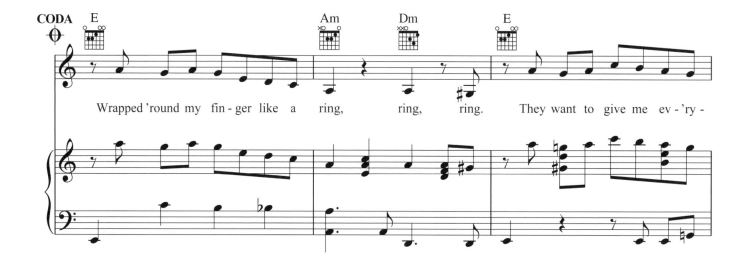

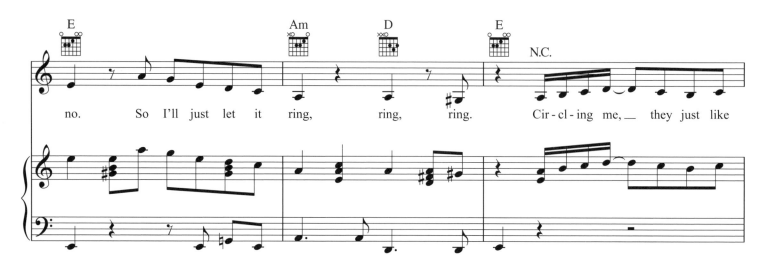

up, they do-ing way too much, so I'll just let it ring, ring, ring.

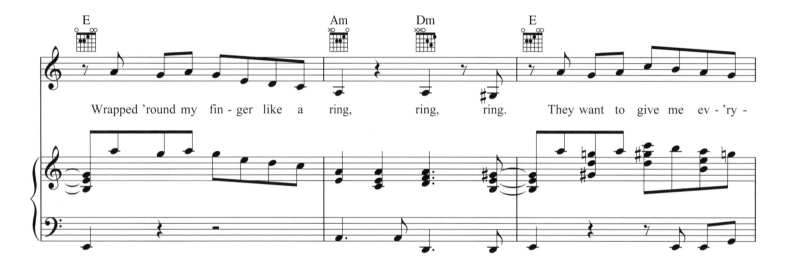

Wrapped 'round my fin-ger like a ring, ring, ring. They want to give me ev-'ry-

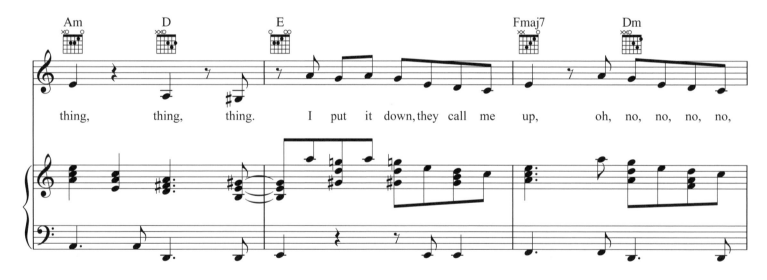

thing, thing, thing. I put it down, they call me up, oh, no, no, no, no,

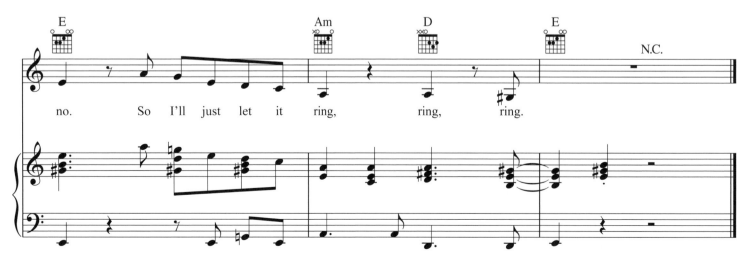

no. So I'll just let it ring, ring, ring.

VULNERABLE

Words and Music by SELENA GOMEZ,
JONATHAN BELLION, STEFAN JOHNSON,
JORDON JOHNSON and AMY ALLEN

Lyrics:

If I give you ev-'ry piece of me, I know that you could drop it.

Give you the chance, I know that you could take ad-van-tage once you got it.

If I o-pen up my heart to you, I know that you could lock it.

Throw a - way the key and keep it there for - ev - er in your pock - et.

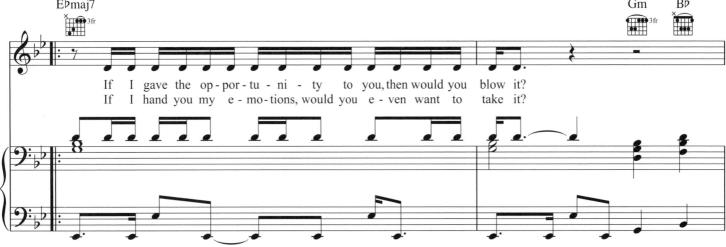

If I gave the op - por - tu - ni - ty to you, then would you blow it?
If I hand you my e - mo - tions, would you e - ven want to take it?

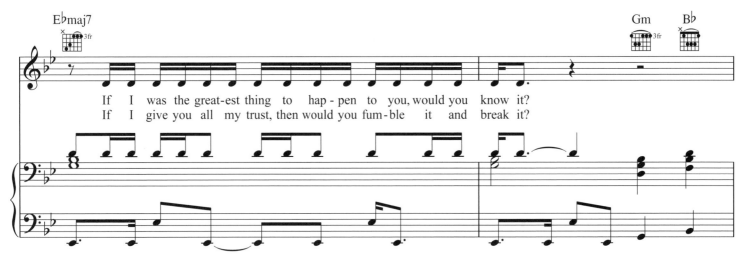

If I was the great - est thing to hap - pen to you, would you know it?
If I give you all my trust, then would you fum - ble it and break it?

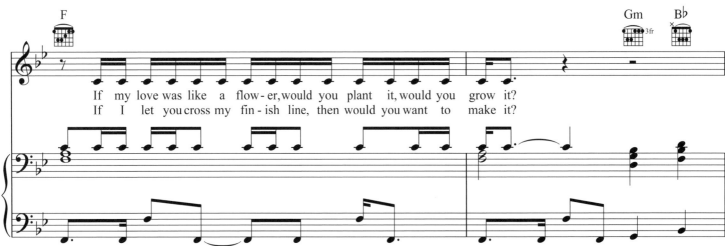

If my love was like a flow - er, would you plant it, would you grow it?
If I let you cross my fin - ish line, then would you want to make it?

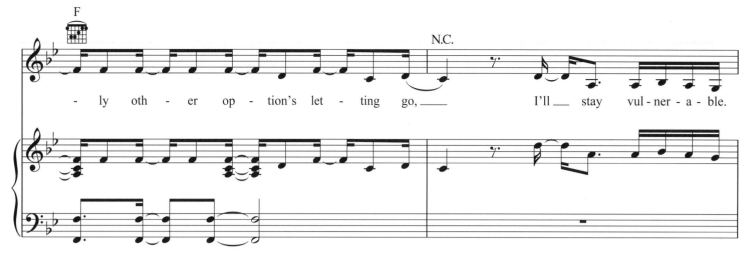

-ly oth - er op - tion's let - ting go, ___ I'll ___ stay vul - ner - a - ble.

Yeah. I'll ___ stay vul - ner - a - ble. Yeah.

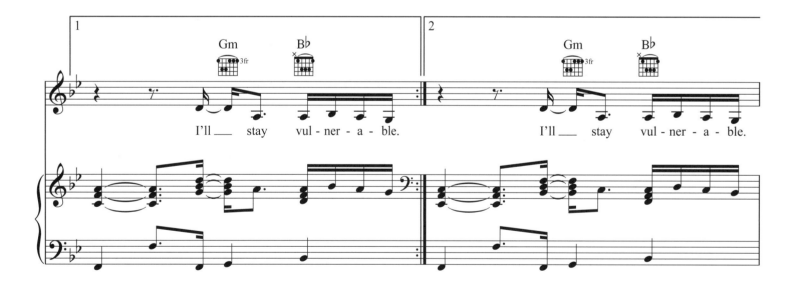

I'll ___ stay vul - ner - a - ble. I'll ___ stay vul - ner - a - ble.

If ___ I show ___

___ you all ___ my de-mons and ___ we dive ___ in-to ___ the deep ___ end, would ___ we crash ___

___ and burn ___ like ev - 'ry time ___ be - fore? _____ I ___ would tell ___

you all my se-crets, wrap your arms a-round my weak-ness. If the on-

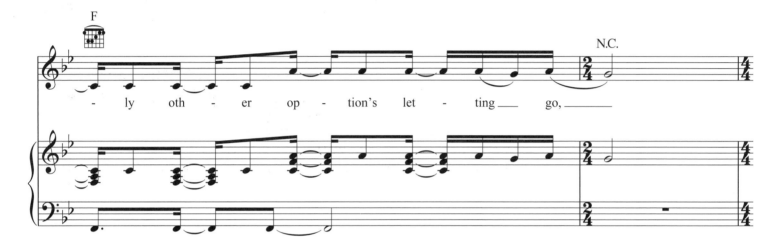

-ly oth-er op-tion's let-ting go,

I'll stay vul-ner-a-ble. Yeah.

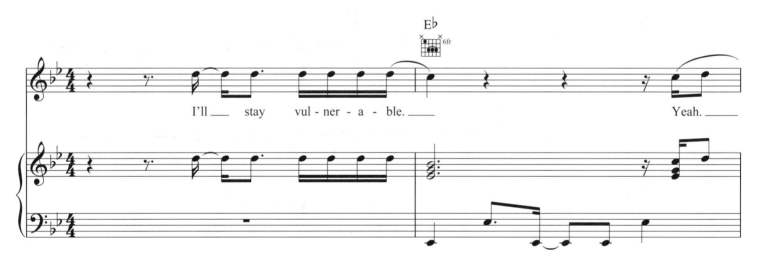

I'll stay vul-ner-a-ble. Yeah, yeah, yeah. If I show

you all my de-mons and we dive in-to the deep end, would we crash

and burn like ev-'ry time be-fore? I would tell

I'll stay vul-ner-a-ble.

you all my sec-rets, wrap your arms a-round my weak-ness. If the on-

-ly oth-er op-tion's let-ting go, I'll stay vul-ner-a-ble.

PEOPLE YOU KNOW

Words and Music by SELENA GOMEZ,
LIL AARON, MATHIEU JOMPHE-LEPINE,
JASON EVIGAN, ALEX HOPE
and STEPH JONES

Moderate Pop Ballad

You were run-ning through me like wa - ter. Now the feel-ing's leav - ing me dry.

These days, we could-n't be far - ther, so how's it feel to be on the oth - er side?

So man-y wast - ed nights with you.

Recorded a half-step lower

I still can taste _ it, I hate ___ it, wish I could take _ it back, _ 'cause:

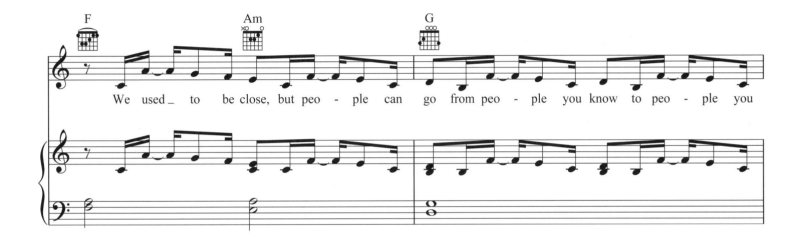

We used _ to be close, but peo - ple can go from peo - ple you know to peo - ple you

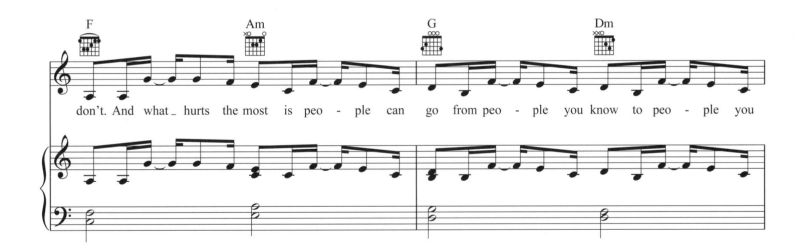

don't. And what _ hurts the most is peo - ple can go from peo - ple you know to peo - ple you

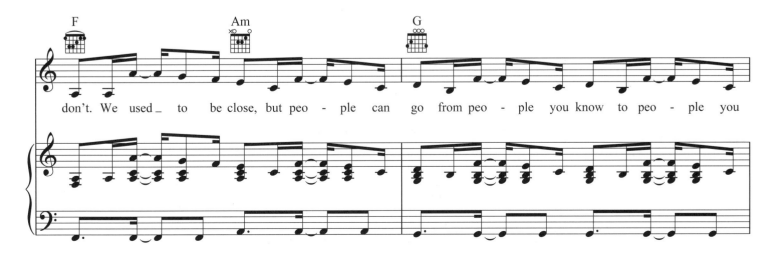

don't. We used _ to be close, but peo - ple can go from peo - ple you know to peo - ple you

don't. And what hurts the most is peo - ple can go from peo - ple you know to peo - ple you

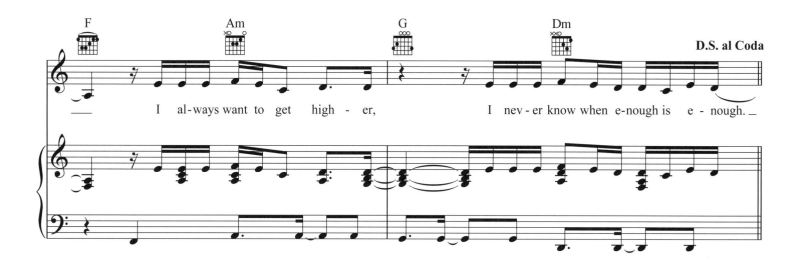

don't. When it was good, we were on fire, now I'm breath - ing ash - es and dust.

I al-ways want to get high - er, I nev - er know when e-nough is e - nough.

go from peo - ple you know to peo - ple you don't. Do do do do do do do do do

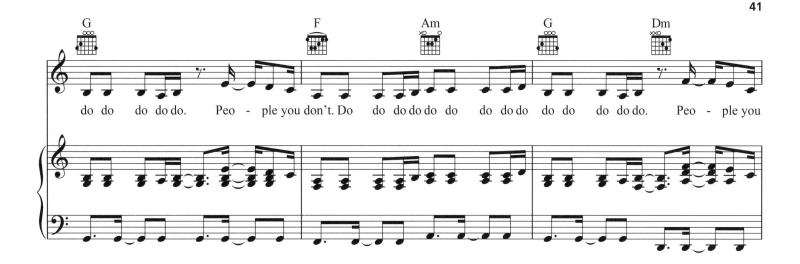

do do do do do. Peo - ple you don't. Do do do do do do do do do do do do do do. Peo - ple you

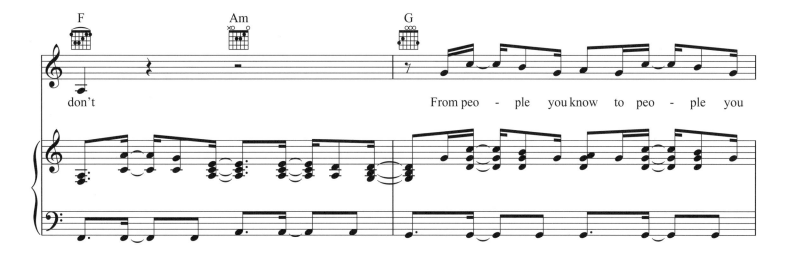

don't

From peo - ple you know to peo - ple you

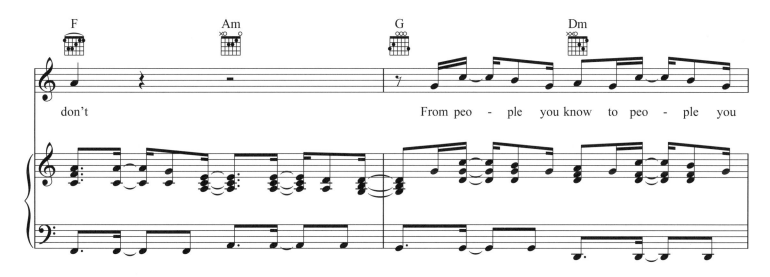

don't

From peo - ple you know to peo - ple you

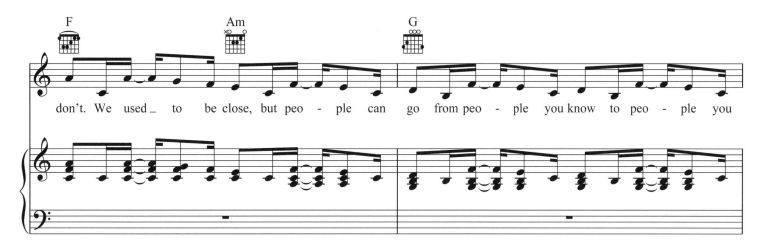

don't. We used _ to be close, but peo - ple can go from peo - ple you know to peo - ple you

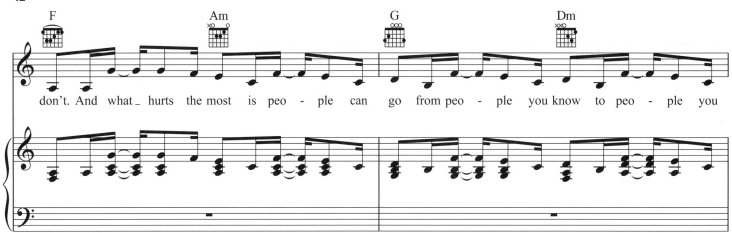

don't. And what _ hurts the most is peo - ple can go from peo - ple you know to peo - ple you

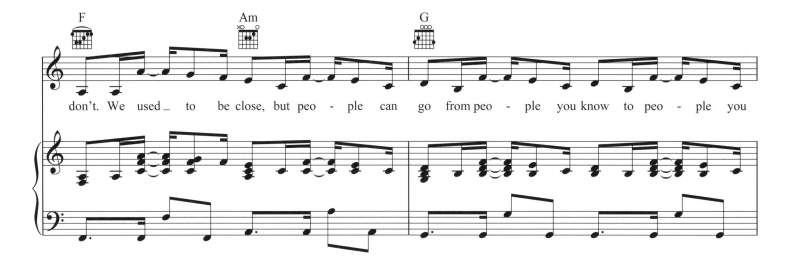

don't. We used _ to be close, but peo - ple can go from peo - ple you know to peo - ple you

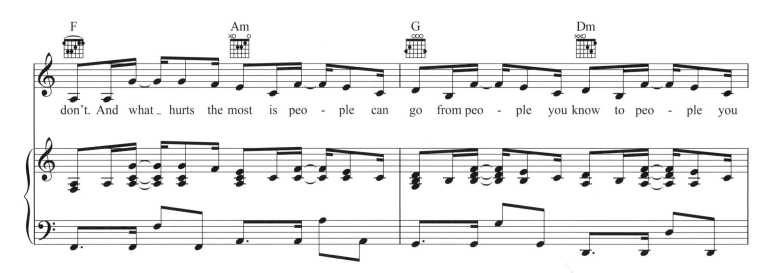

don't. And what _ hurts the most is peo - ple can go from peo - ple you know to peo - ple you

don't. Do do do do do do do do do do. From peo - ple you know to peo - ple you

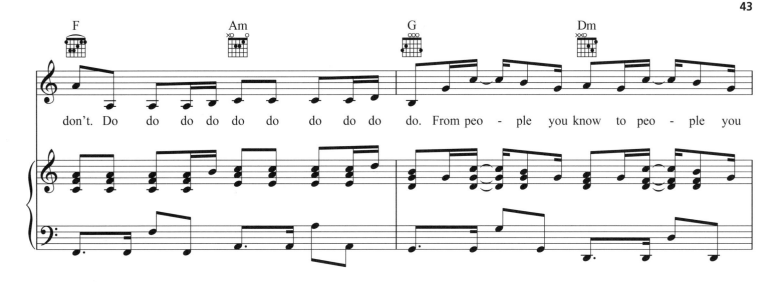

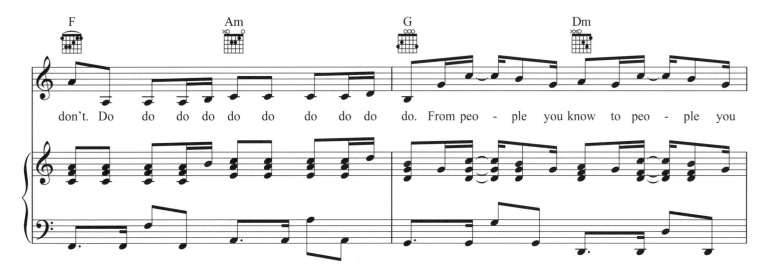

LET ME GET ME

Words and Music by SELENA GOMEZ,
ROBIN FREDRIKSSON, MATTIAS LARSSON,
JUSTIN TRANTER and CAROLINE AILIN

Latin-flavored Dance beat

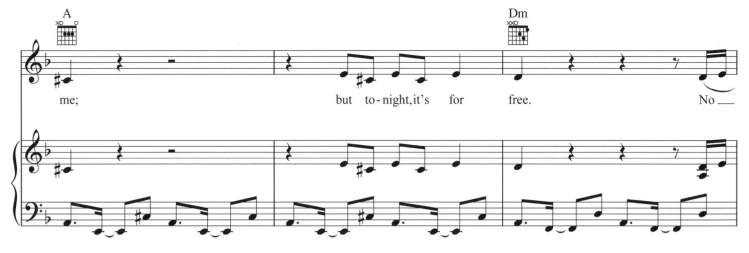

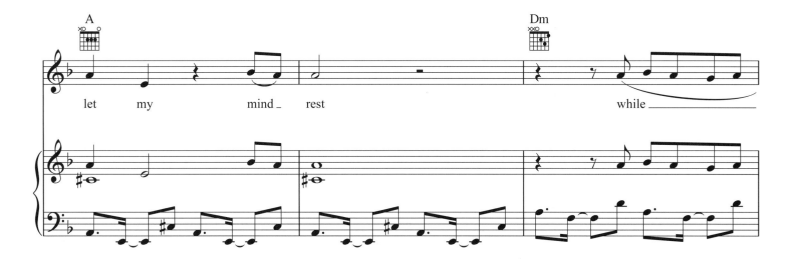

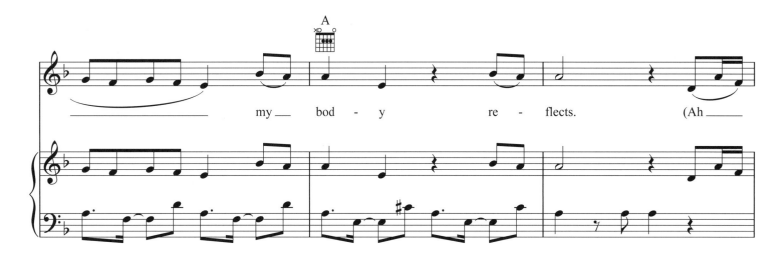

I won't let me get me. (Ah ___ ooh.) ___ I'm good right now. ___ I won't let me get me.

Take that ti-red heart and move and turn it in - side... ___ out. _____ Div-ing

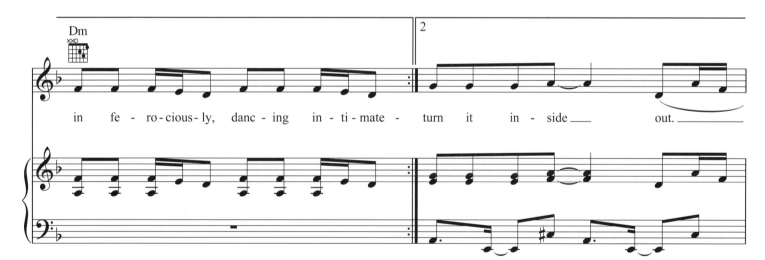

in fe-ro-cious-ly, danc-ing in-ti-mate - turn it in-side ___ out. ___

_____ Don't get me down. _

turn it in - side... ___ Oh

my,   I guess this is what it feels like to be free. (Ooh.) _____
my,   I guess this is what if feels like to see me. (Ooh.) _____

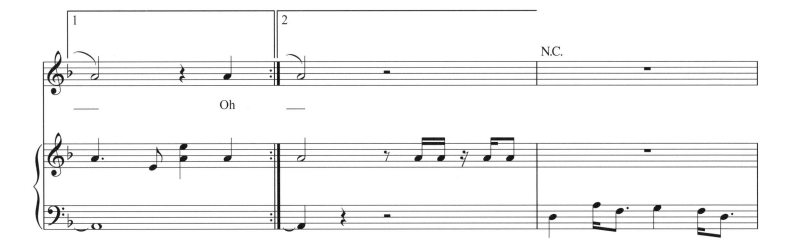

_____   Oh _____

(Get down.) Don't get me (down.) _____   (Get

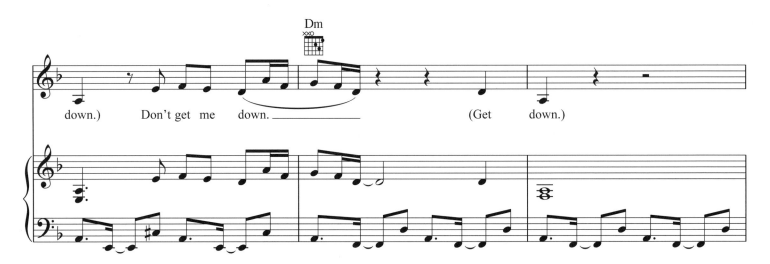

down.) Don't get me down. _____   (Get down.)

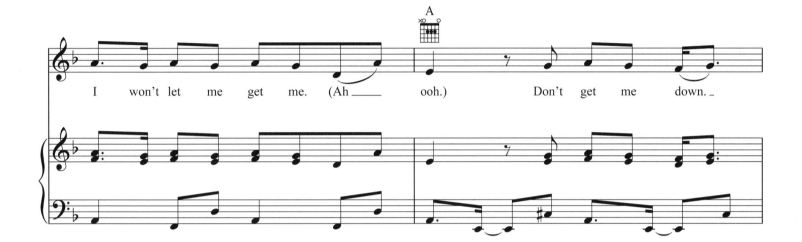

CROWDED ROOM

Words and Music by SELENA GOMEZ,
RICORDO VALENTINE, BLETA REXHA,
NOLAN LAMBROZA, SIMON ROSEN
and SIMON WILCOX

Moderately slow groove

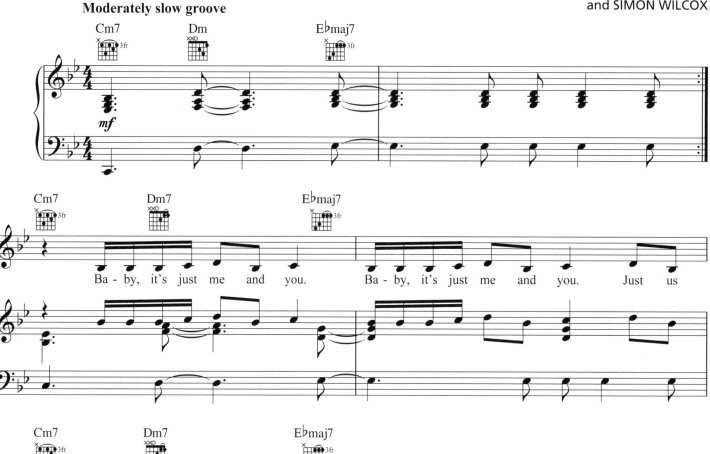

Ba - by, it's just me and you. Ba - by, it's just me and you. Just us

two, e - ven in a crowd - ed room. Ba - by, it's just me and you, yeah.

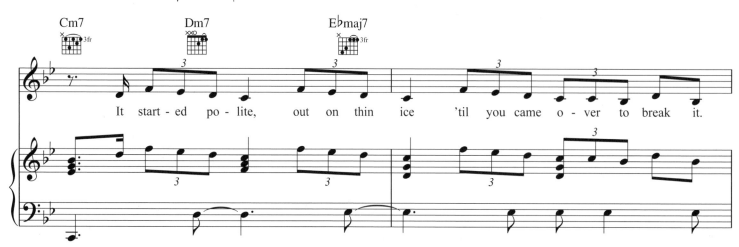

It start - ed po - lite, out on thin ice 'til you came o - ver to break it.

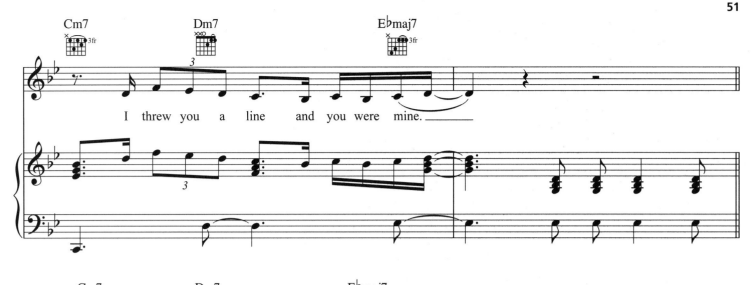

I threw you a line and you were mine. _____

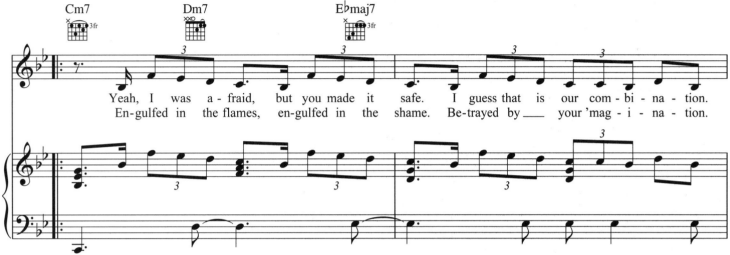

Yeah, I was a-fraid, but you made it safe. I guess that is our com-bi-na-tion.
En-gulfed in the flames, en-gulfed in the shame. Be-trayed by ____ your 'mag-i-na-tion.

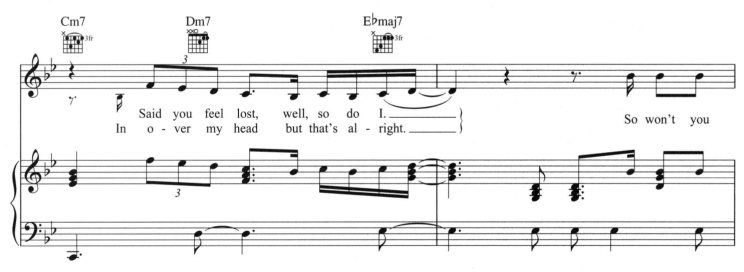

Said you feel lost, well, so do I. _____
In o-ver my head but that's al-right. _____
So won't you

call me in the morn-in'? I think that you should call me in the morn-in' if you

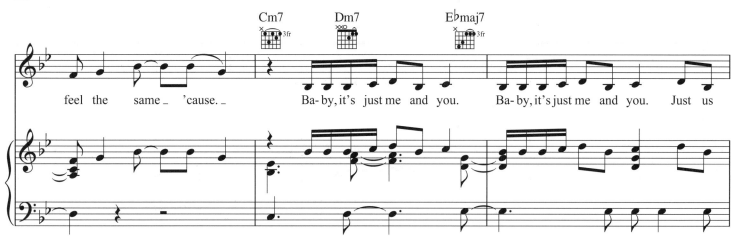

feel the same __ 'cause. __ Ba - by, it's just me and you. Ba - by, it's just me and you. Just us

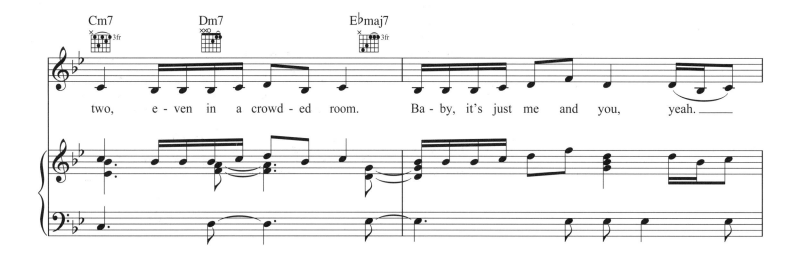

two, e - ven in a crowd - ed room. Ba - by, it's just me and you, yeah. _____

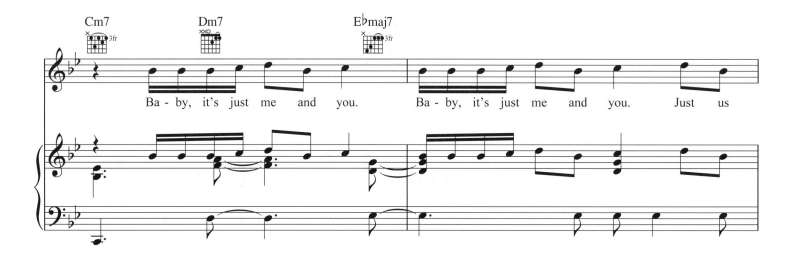

Ba - by, it's just me and you. Ba - by, it's just me and you. Just us

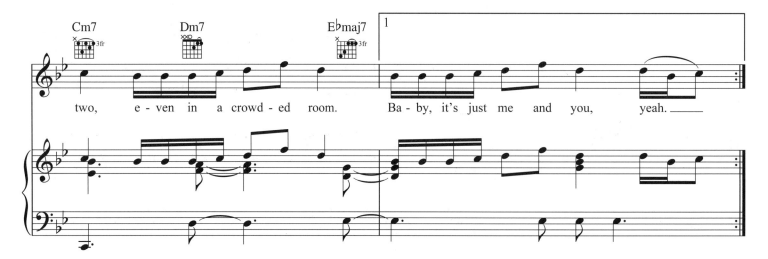

two, e - ven in a crowd - ed room. Ba - by, it's just me and you, yeah. _____

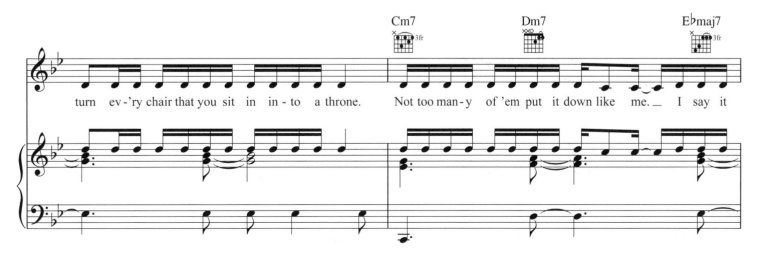

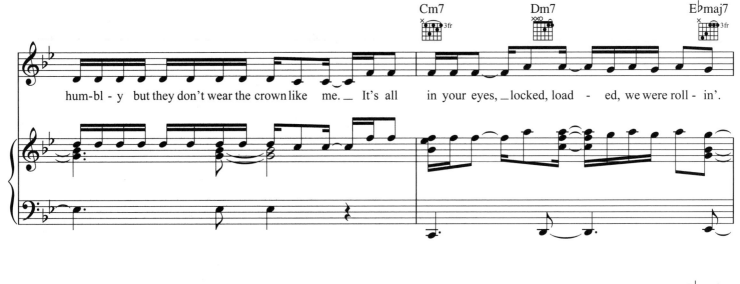

hum-bl-y but they don't wear the crown like me. __ It's all in your eyes, __ locked, load - ed, we were roll - in'.

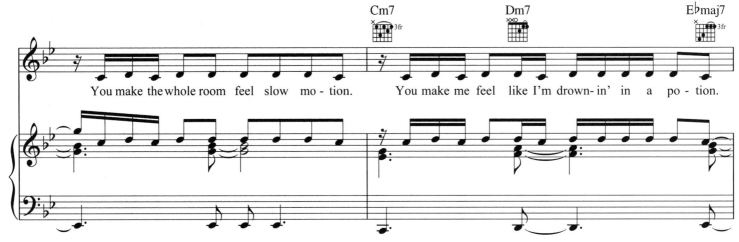

You make the whole room feel slow mo - tion. You make me feel like I'm drown-in' in a po - tion.

Closed off, try'n-a get a lit-tle o - pen. The more that I give, the more that I

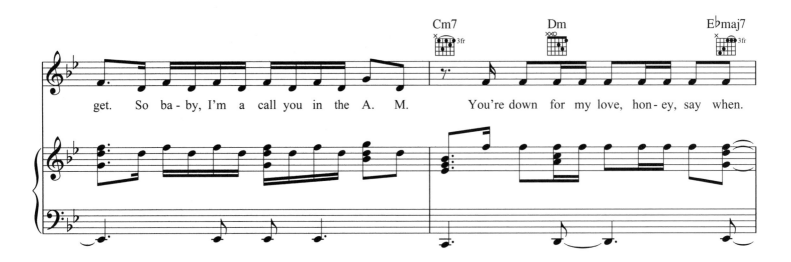

get. So ba-by, I'm a call you in the A. M. You're down for my love, hon-ey, say when.

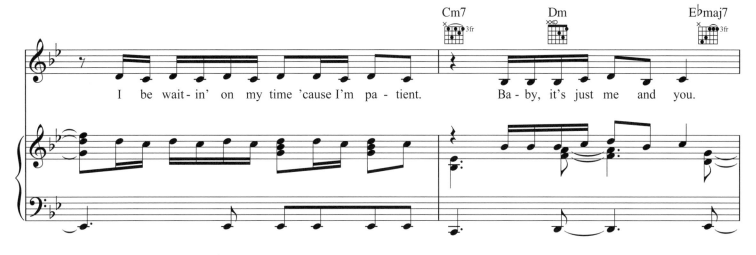

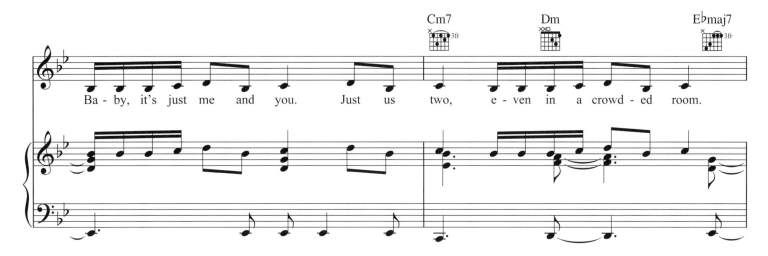

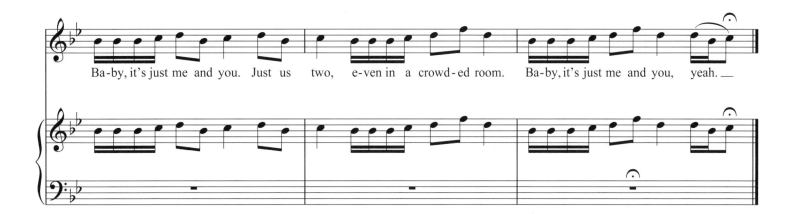

KINDA CRAZY

Words and Music by SELENA GOMEZ,
JASMINE THOMPSON, ALBIN NEDLER,
KRISTOFFER FOGELMARK, RAMI YACOUB
and JUSTIN TRANTER

16th note Shuffle

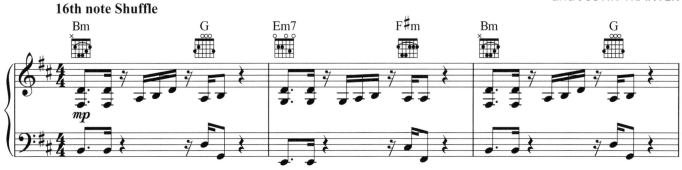

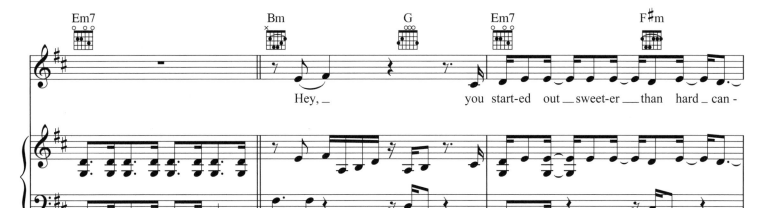

Hey, __ you start-ed out __ sweet-er __ than hard __ can-

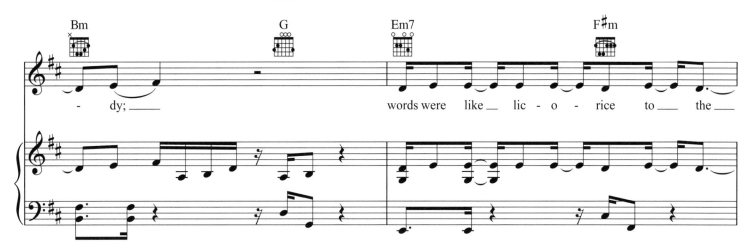

-dy; ___ words were like __ lic-o-rice to __ the __

__ taste. __ But slow-ly, all __ the sug-ar, it went to __

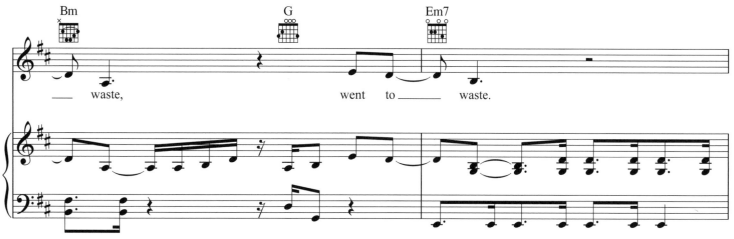

waste, went to _____ waste.

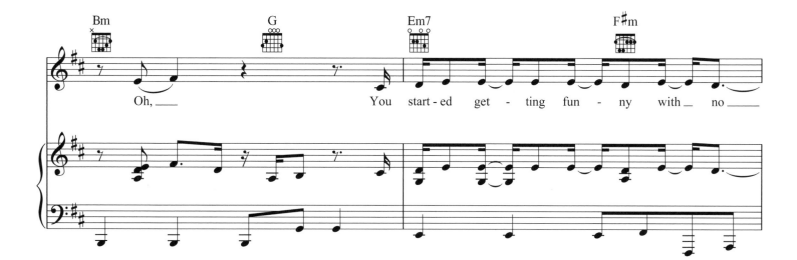

Oh, _____ You start-ed get-ting fun-ny with __ no _____

_____ jokes. __ I start-ed see-ing through __ you like __ a

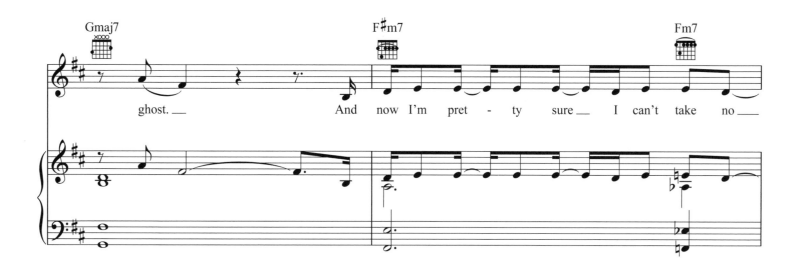

ghost. __ And now I'm pret-ty sure __ I can't take no _____

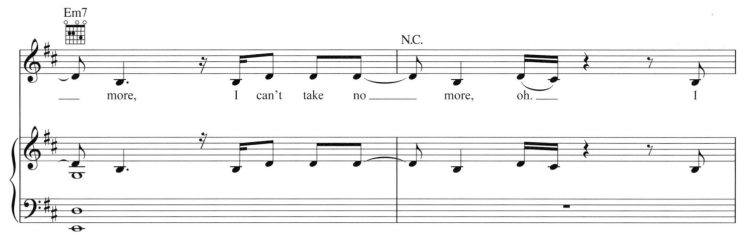

more, I can't take no ___ more, oh. ___ I

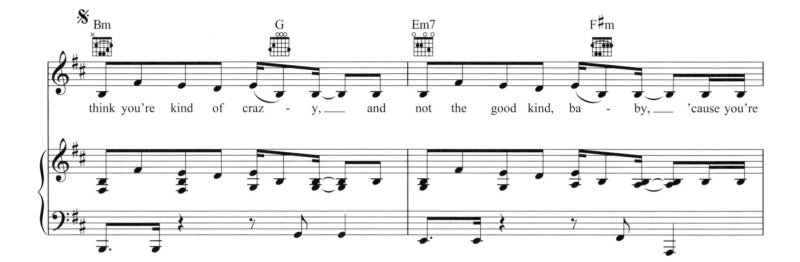

think you're kind of craz - y, ___ and not the good kind, ba - by, ___ 'cause you're

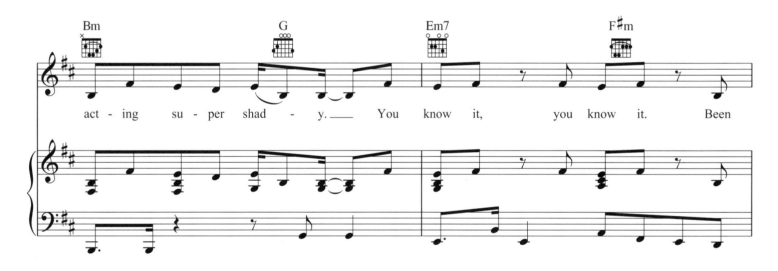

act - ing su - per shad - y. ___ You know it, you know it. Been

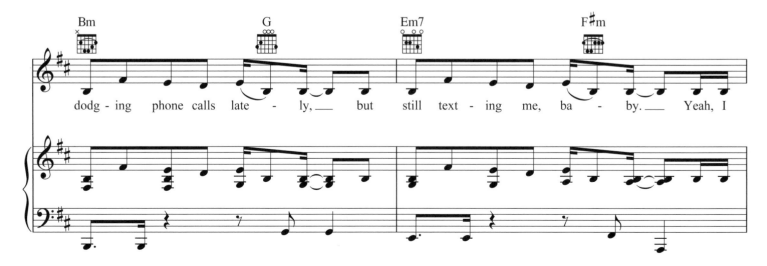

dodg - ing phone calls late - ly, ___ but still text - ing me, ba - by. ___ Yeah, I

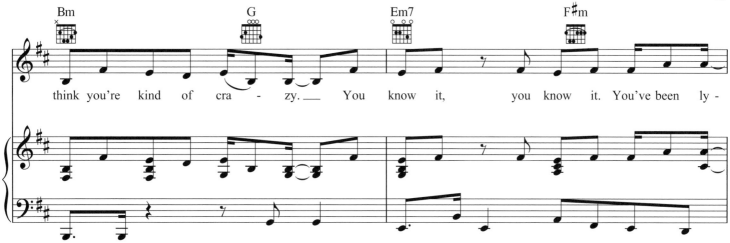

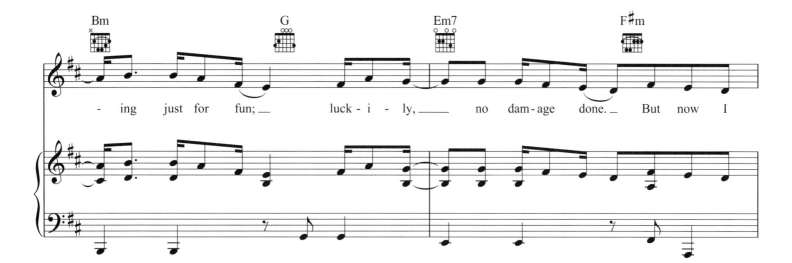

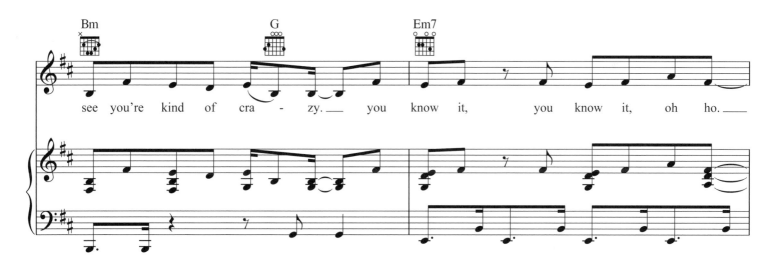

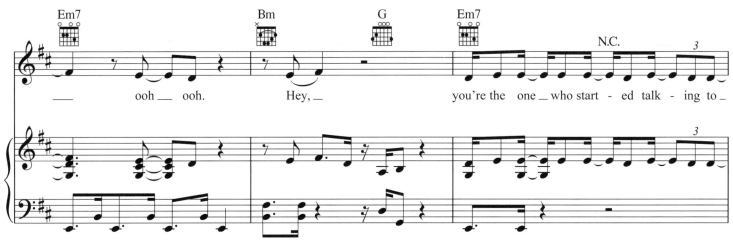

ooh __ ooh. Hey, __ you're the one __ who start - ed talk - ing to __

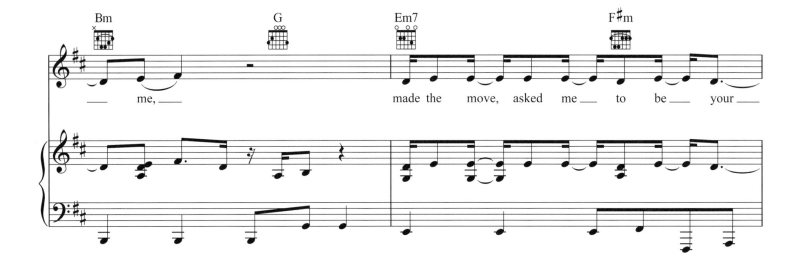

__ me, __ made the move, asked me __ to be __ your __

__ babe. __ And now you're treat - ing me __ like I'm __ in -

- sane. You're in - sane. _____ I

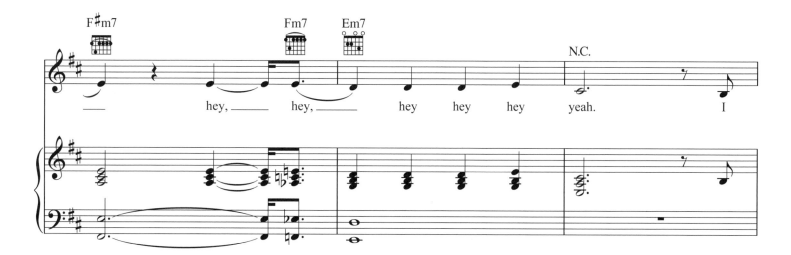

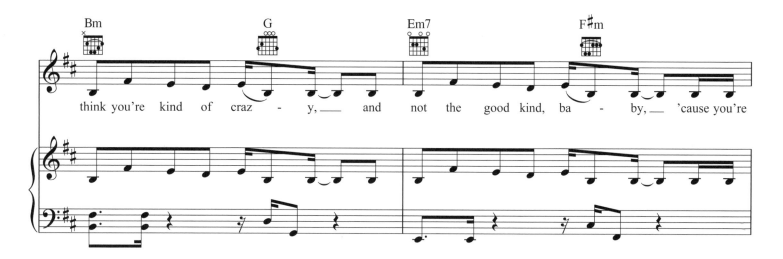

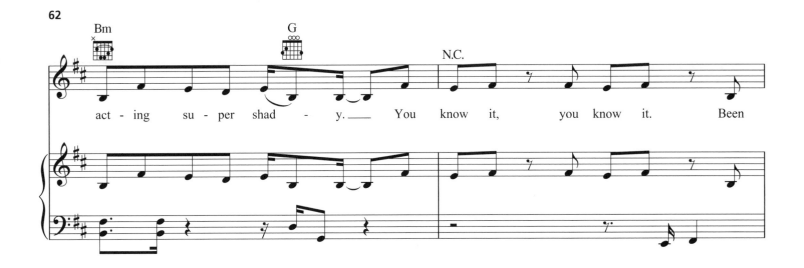

act- ing su- per shad - y.___ You know it, you know it. Been

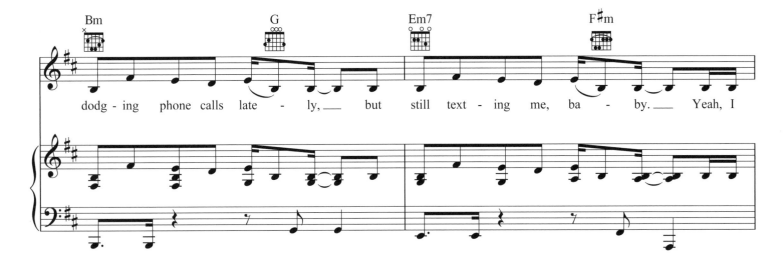

dodg- ing phone calls late - ly,___ but still text- ing me, ba - by.___ Yeah, I

think you're kind of cra - zy.___ You know it, you know it, oh ho.____ Oh ho __

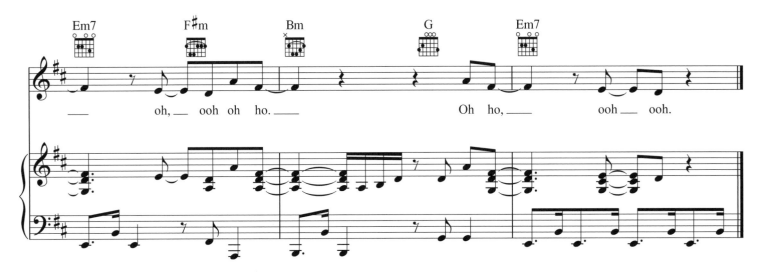

__ oh, __ ooh oh ho.___ Oh ho, ___ ooh __ ooh.

CUT YOU OFF

Words and Music by SELENA GOMEZ,
LIZA OWEN, CHLOE ANGELIDES
and DAVID PRAMIK

Slow Groove

Pull up to the mir - ror, star - ing at my face. Got - ta chop, chop all the ex - tra weight I've been car - ry - in' for four - teen hun - dred six - ty days. Got - ta, got - ta, got - ta clean my slate. And I might as well just tell you while I'm

drunk, yeah. The truth is that I think I've had e - nough

(pro -
(e -

fes - sion - al - ly mess - in' with my trust.)
mo - tion - al - ly mess - in' with my health.)

How could I con - fuse that shit for

love? So I got - ta get ___ you ___ out my head now, I just

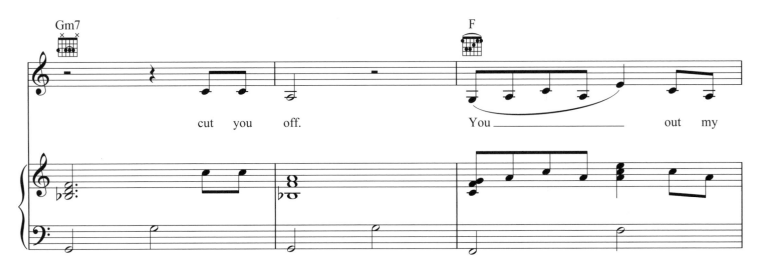

cut you off. You ___ out my

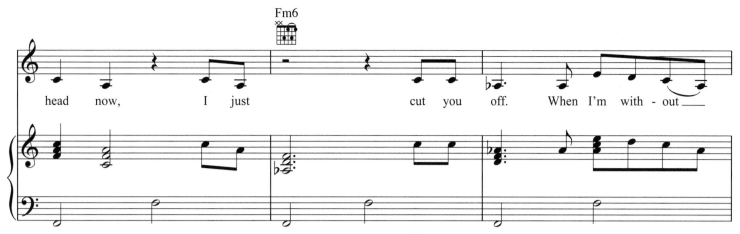

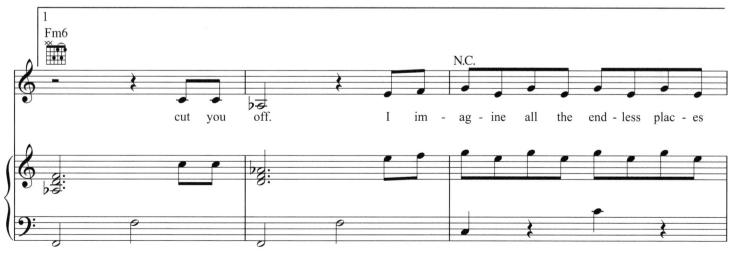

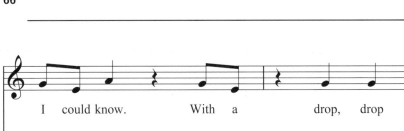

I could know. With a drop, drop and I'll let you go. All the

pos - si - bil - i - ties I got from head to toe. Yeah, they'd, yeah, they'd, yeah, they'd

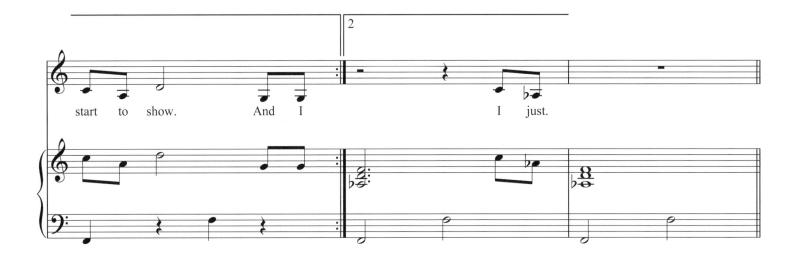

start to show. And I I just.

(Guitar solo ad lib. on repeat.)

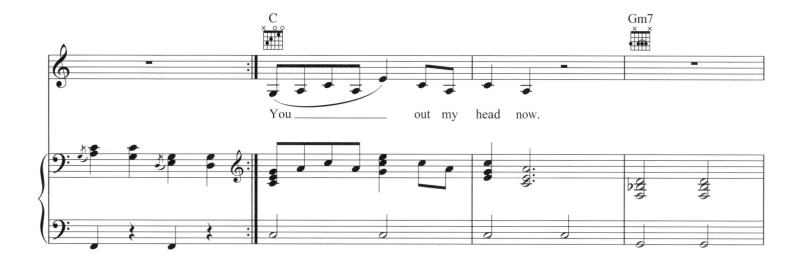

You _____ out my head now.

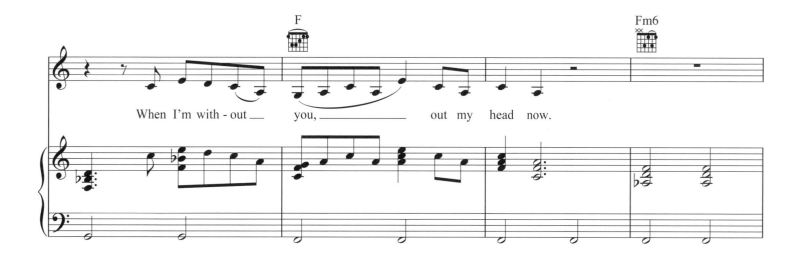

When I'm with-out ___ you, _____ out my head now.

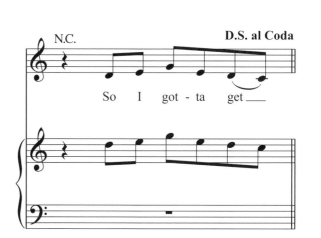

So I got-ta get ___

I just, yeah.

FUN

Words and Music by SELENA GOMEZ,
RAUL CUBINA, SCOTT HARRIS,
JULIA MICHAELS and MARK WILLIAMS

Dance groove

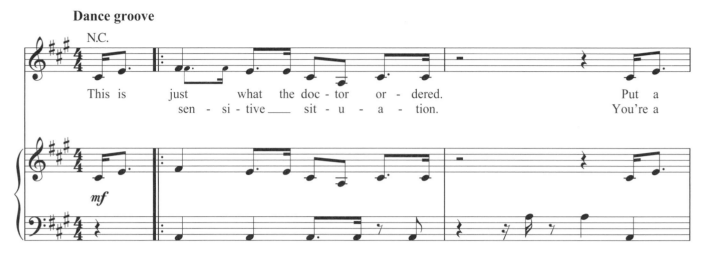

This is just what the doc-tor or-dered. Put a
sen-si-tive___ sit-u-a-tion. You're a

gold star on my dis-or-der. Yeah, we've
hot and cold___ com-bi-na-tion. Oh, we

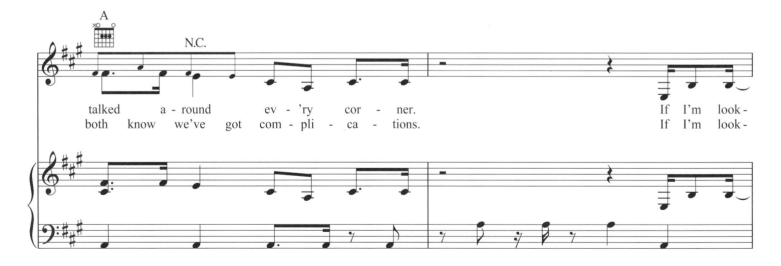

talked a-round ev-'ry cor-ner. If I'm look-
both know we've got com-pli-ca-tions. If I'm look-

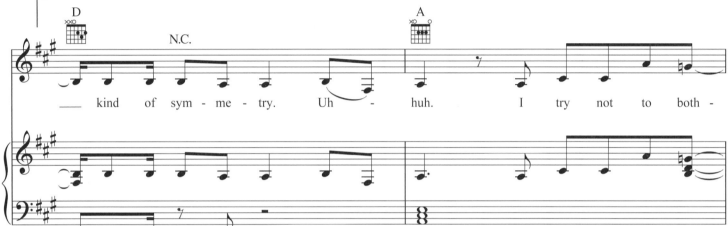

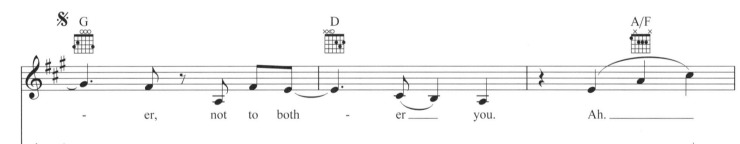

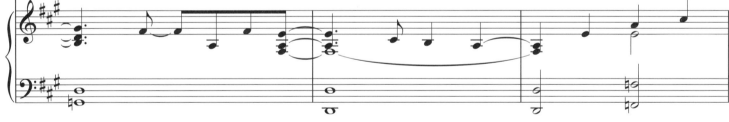

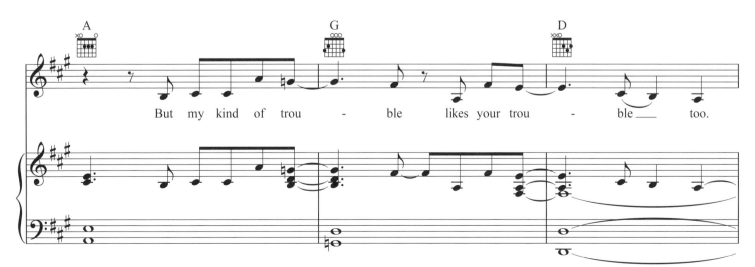

Can't stop my-self, it's true. I like the way you move, uh-huh. Oh, __ we got some-thing in this room, can't make that up. You may not be the one, uh-huh, but you look like fun. Oh oh oh, oh oh oh. I like the way you

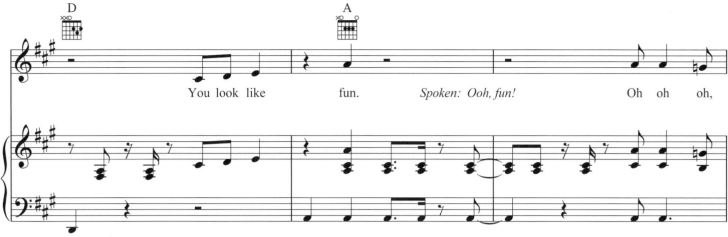

You look like fun. *Spoken: Ooh, fun!* Oh oh oh,

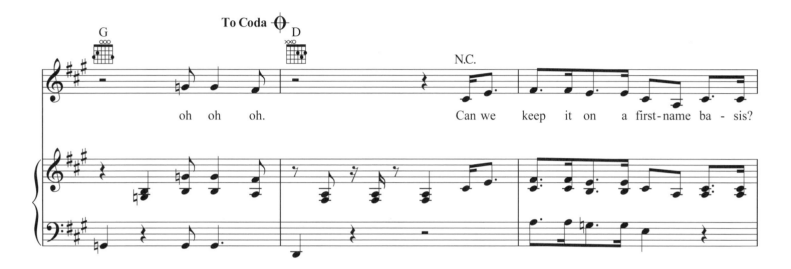

oh oh oh. Can we keep it on a first-name ba - sis?

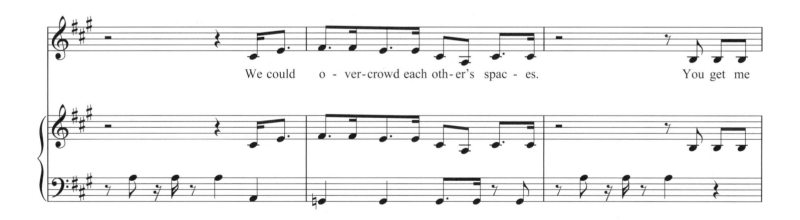

We could o - ver-crowd each oth-er's spac - es. You get me

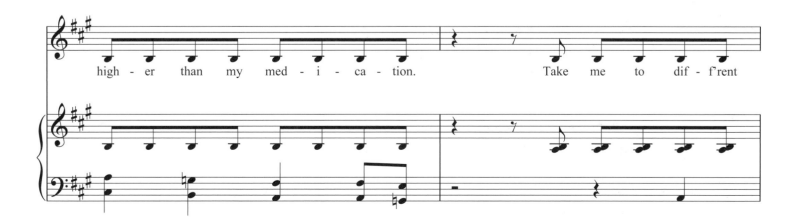

high - er than my med - i - ca - tion. Take me to dif - f'rent

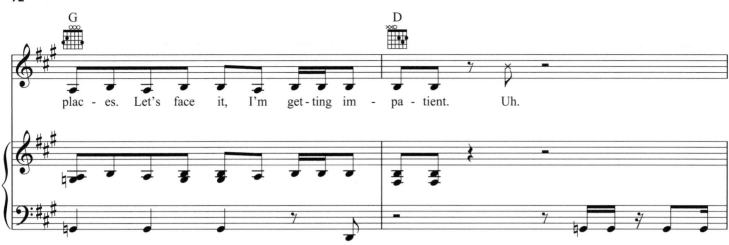

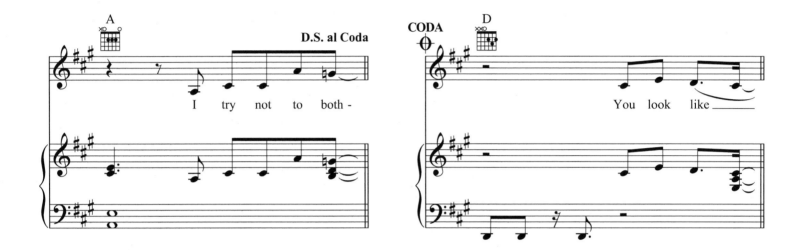

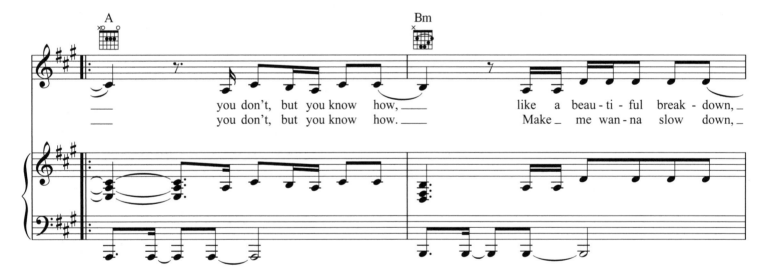

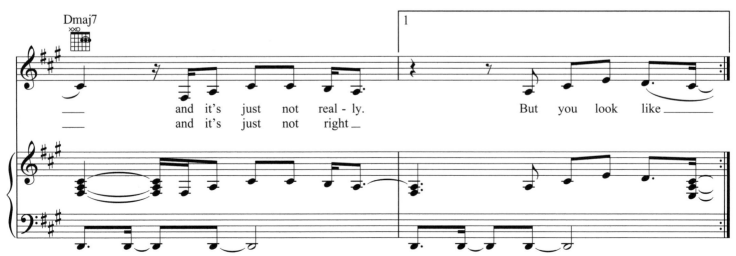

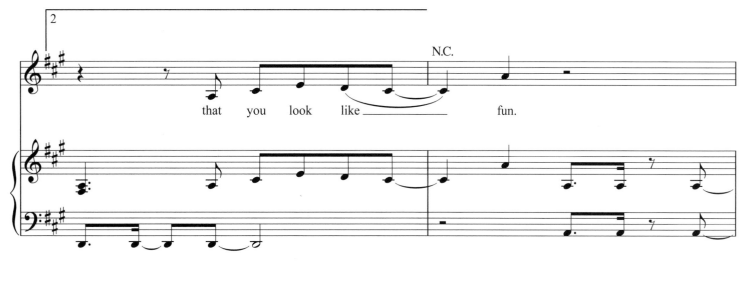

that you look like _____ fun.

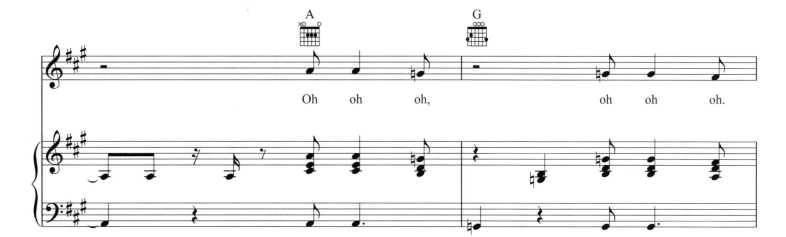

Oh oh oh, oh oh oh.

You look like fun. *Ooh, fun!* Oh oh oh,

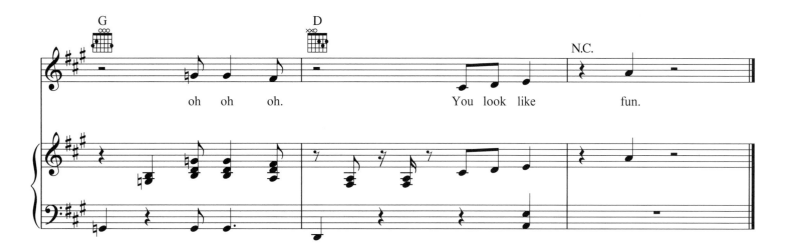

oh oh oh. You look like fun.

A SWEETER PLACE

Words and Music by SELENA GOMEZ,
IAN KIRKPATRICK, MADISON LOVE,
KID CUDI and UZOECHI EMENIKE

* Recorded a half step lower.

Sweet-er place, _____ there must be a sweet-er.

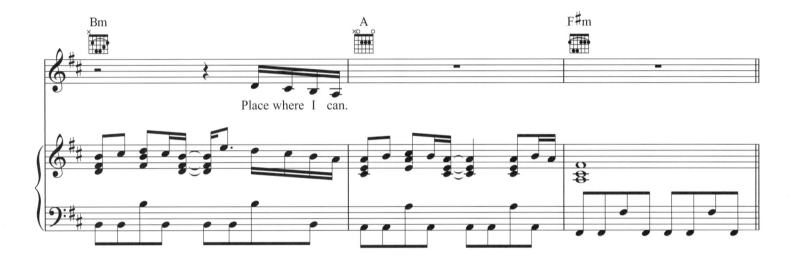

Place where I can.

Ooh, _____ you real-ly wan-na know where I've been all this time?

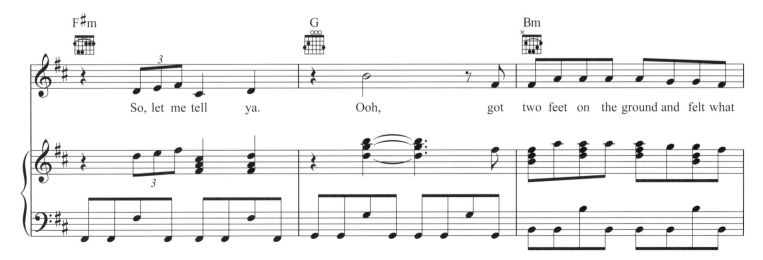

So, let me tell ya. Ooh, _____ got two feet on the ground and felt what

real is like.   What it was like   liv - in' __ out of __ the scene,

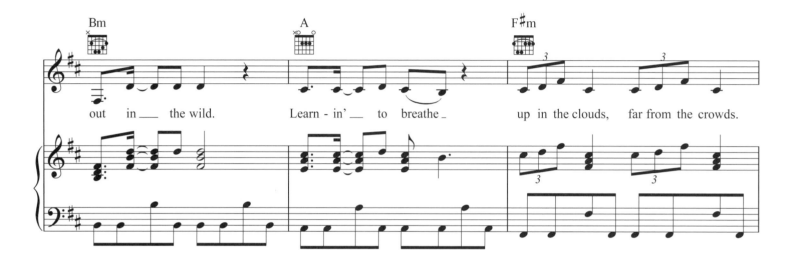

out in __ the wild.   Learn - in' __ to breathe __   up in the clouds,   far from the crowds.

I can't __ be-lieve   I can __ be loud. __   Hold-in' hands with the dark-ness and know-in' my heart is al-

lowed,   al - lowed. _____   Is there a place where I can hide a - way?

Red lips, French kiss my wor-ries all a - way. There must be a sweet - er place.

We can sug-ar coat _ the taste. _ Sweet - er place, _ there must be a sweet-er

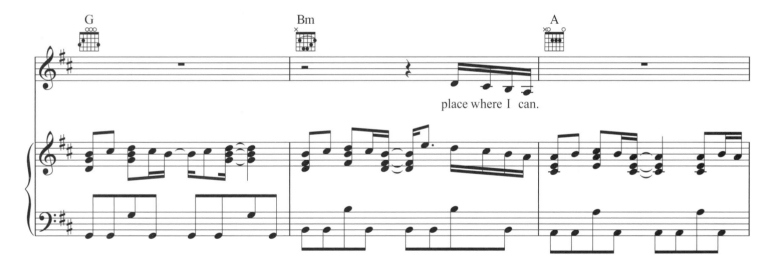

place where I can.

Place where I can.

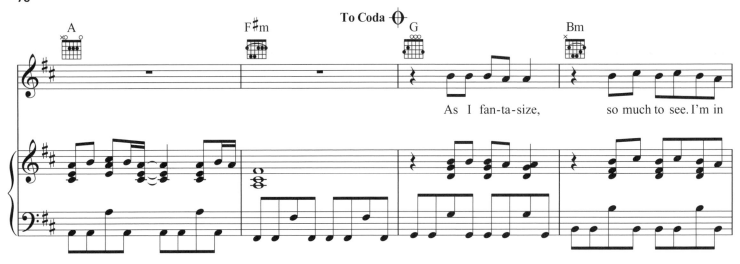

See, I'm mes-mer-ized. This is just for me and I am

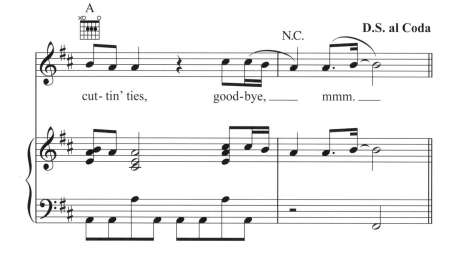

cut-tin' ties, good-bye, ___ mmm. ___

Have no fear, heav-en is

near, oh __ whoa. __ Head is so clear. A sweet-er place, my sweet-er place. ___

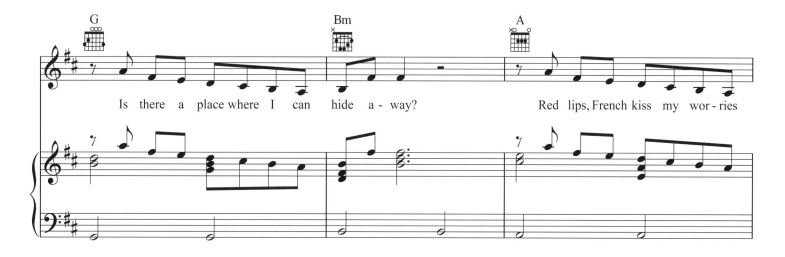

Is there a place where I can hide a-way? Red lips, French kiss my wor-ries

all a-way. There must be a sweet-er place.__ We can sug-ar coat__ the taste.__

Sweet-er place,__ there must be a sweet-er

place where I can. Ooh._____